Rainbow Sky Poetry

Celia Markham

BOOKBILDR PUBLISHING

First published in the USA in 2025 by BookBildr Publishing.

The moral rights of the author and illustrator have been asserted.

ISBN 978-1-964012-56-8

BookBildr Publishing

An imprint of BookBildr LLC

7901 4th St N, Suite 300

St. Petersburg, FL, 33702

USA

www.bookbildr.com

Other Books by Celia Markham

Blue Butterfly Poems

Nature Photography

Bandit & King A Tale of Two Brothers

Lollipop and Cleo A Sister Story

Never take your dreams to bed

And leave them hanging in the night

Never blow your candles out and

Wish that they were burning bright

Always hear and do what's said

Never take your dreams to bed

At 2 pm I was happy

And I slept and dreamt

It was 5 pm

And I thought I'd be happy

But I missed 2 pm

And I thought

So is my life

The dawn and then

The day

And last

The night

And when the day is over

I'll miss the day

But I'll be happy

In the night

Sadness can be a hard habit to break

Always it comes with a familiar ache

Even if sadness no longer suits

Arguing with it is pointedly moot

Like running through fire to avoid the flame

Or feeling deflated ahead of the game

A frown is a furrow where dark feelings burrow

And still sadness comes even though it's unbidden

To stir up the hurts that you thought were well hidden

But sadness sometimes is so easy to break

Like leaves from my garden that cling to my rake

Like chocolate in boxes and frosting

On cake

With glue and some paper

Now happiness make

I am Music in human form

My guitar and I are safe and warm

My body rises with my song

I am Art for all the ages

All the stages and mazes of my heart

Of the Art I am a part

I am Love entwined in laughter

And after, I am Love in a bottle

Lightening in a blaze

I am Life in my essence

I have colors in my presence

I am Joy undeniable

And Grace it is reliable

All is me, I am all

I am every thought I have ever seen

Every dream I have ever dreamed

Every light that has ever beamed

I am like Sleeping Beauty

I'd been given many gifts

But the pricking of my finger

Was the doubt upon my lips

I doubted I was worthy

I doubted I was smart

I felt that I was bankrupt

Disconnected from my art

My lonely tower hovered

The walls grown thick with thorns

I waded into darkness

And then I was reborn

My Prince he scaled the tower

My Prince he held me tight

I felt that I was lucky

As the day passed into night

Outside there are new roses

New songs and new ideas

Outside the sun is shining

On the way that I now feel

I was like Sleeping Beauty

But now I am just fine

Awake, alert, and always

I am doubtless all the time

We made a commitment

To the here and now

But our future selves

Are wondering how

To bridge the gap

To live exultant

Alive, thriving, joy, exultant

In perfect peace, in perfect health

And not a pawn

For the unchecked self

The self that knows

The path is slim

Can't be out if you want to be in

The soul that asks, "Take care of me?"

The body that acts out flagrantly

Alive, thriving, joy, exultant

Alive, thrive, joy, exult

The past is over now

Just the dust on the rim of an old wine cup

I dreamt of visions and with every image

Shredded through my past

A squabbled history

But now my happiness

It's not a mystery

The sun is shining now

The past is over now

Just the trace of the cobwebs after the broom swept by

I felt so violently

And with every feeling

Squeezing out my past

A scattered history

But now my happiness

It's not a mystery

The sun is shining now

It's hard to catch a memory

They spin out so fast

Water through your fingers or

Sands through the hourglass but

I remember, I remember, I do

Dancing for Erin in the kitchen

Swirling my skirt to Spanish music

Unfinished cookie dough waiting in trays on the table

And my little Erin, bright eyed infant

Dancing back at me

Smiling and shaking little hands and fist

And I remember, I remember, I do

I remember thinking

"Life really doesn't get any better than this"

As we go out into the morning

About the light and leaves

A breath of ice will disappear

Leave a trace upon our coats

We smile for no good reason

Living souls in a dying town

The moon rose up

The sun went down

We missed it rise

But it's enough

A new moment is upon us

And it is different than the last

It came upon us slowly

Like the future always does

So that we have not noticed

"Never stay in one place!" the woman said to me

She sat upon the park bench and preached Eternity

There was hell and fire and brimstone flaming from her soul

She jumped up on her old brown shoes and gathered up her clothes

An old red scarf fell on the road

She stopped and she bent down

She saw me watch her walk away

And said, "What are you still doing in this here town?"

I turned and walked the other way

A bus pulled into town

I hear she's down in Mexico

Chasing the devil down

Hats

Today I packed your hats away

They smelled of you

They smelled of you

And all the time I packed was brave

To give away

To give away

And all the time I thought of you

Now Worlds away

Now Worlds away

Today I packed your hats away

And cried because I am so brave

To be without your hats today

My Father's raincoat is a place to hide

From all the storms that won't subside

It's cool or warm

It's close

It shines

With happy memories left behind

And when I feel it's all too much

And I am lost and out of touch

I see his raincoat open wide

And hear his welcome,

"Step inside"

"Believe that you are all you need"

"As I believe in you, Believe"

And when my hiding time is through

I feel new strength and hope anew

I see myself through Father's eyes

I'm good and fair

And kind and wise

And never am I all alone

My father's there and I am home

I am my mother's memory

She is delighted with the scenes

I tell her

I am my mother's memory

Weaving words

Telling tales

Her face alights

Her eyes amazed

And sometimes nods and smiles

At the Grace of Faith again

I am my mother's memory

I help her see the life

She breathes

So this is how people lose their identities

Although I do feel very much myself

It's when you get caught in the spider web

Lost in the memory

That you get hurt

And if I've been kidding myself, I apologize

You know, for what it's worth

It's just on rainy days

I get melancholy

Rain dripping on my shirt

So this is how people lose their identities

Although in the last few days I've been kidding myself

You know, for what it's worth

A clenched fist tightly held

Can't hold a lollipop

It can't feel the sun

On the lines of its palm

It doesn't know what day it is

It hurts when I open it

Unused to the night air

A clenched heart is worse

My friend

A crushed petal underfoot

God's hand is very big

He holds my tiny fist in his

He hopes that I can

Feel his palm

He helps that I can open mine

A clenched fist doesn't let you

Love someone

It doesn't hear

The words of songs

It doesn't know which way

Is out

It doesn't know what

life's about

Thank God you came into my life

Holding out your hand

Cool and crisp in the night air

My hand is opening now

Do you think that I will dance again

And would you believe

that I'm holding your hand

Open up, let me in

A clenched fist

Never again

I cry for you most all day long

I cry for you

And the wind blows on

I want to rest and sing a song

I want to rest

And the wind blows on

I want to do right and never do wrong

I want to do right

And the wind blows on

Time takes me away

From all things I wish to forget

Time brings me closer

To the times that I've wished for

Holds me in its sleeve

Sees me hide my face in it

Forgive and Forget

The forgiving is easier

I think

Which brings me back to Time

Frozen like a lake

I don't want

To skate back there

Anymore

I remember

Where that icy patch was

The one I broke

Fell into drowning

The sting of the water

And how I was saved

I put up a sign

No Trespassing

And refused to slide

On that ice again

Time is my hero

Time is my friend

Time brought me love

And life unfroze again

The Death of Peter Pan

So much promise

Wrapped in so much pain

He can't fly to Neverland

His wings are broken

A sunny smile and a

Wave of his hand

And in your mind

He's in Neverland again

We remember

Peter Pan

Engaging smile and

Heart in Hand

A favorite pal for all the boys

Spreading secrets and glitter

And pixie joys

Charming enough to fool

Captain Hook

Charming the girls

With one brown eyed look

Raise a Toast to Peter Pan

He never grew up

In his Neverland

He left us all here to grow

Old and grey

He took his pixie dust

When he went away

So much promise

Wrapped in so much pain

He'll never come back

To see us again

But deep in your heart

And mind he will stay

The golden boy

For all of your days

I understand now what Grown Up means

I grew

I grew

I stumbled I fell

I saw my reflection

As a three-year-old child and

I'm still out in the sun

Blunder Blunder

In the night

I hold on to my soul very tight

And finally

All I can say

When speaking to

The mixed-up past is

Thank You

I am an artist

And the children are my paint

My oils and my watercolors

I am an artist

And I mix it all together

So clear and so quaint

To form a rainbow

The palette, the masterpiece

Sometimes the colors are muddled and faint

Sometimes the colors just slip off the page

I curse and I wander around in a rage

But oh

All the pictures

I've managed to paint.

ABOUT THE AUTHOR

Celia Markham is a mixed media artist and painter.

She is a mother, a teacher, a singer, and a poet.

She hopes you will find inspiration and joy in this book.

RAINBOW SKY POETRY

January 2025